THIS BOOK
BELONGS TO

....

Other books by Nick Butterworth and Mick Inkpen:

THE NATIVITY PLAY
SCHOOL TRIP
JUST LIKE JASPER!
JASPER'S BEANSTALK

Copyright © Nick Butterworth and Mick Inkpen 1988
The rights of Nick Butterworth and Mick Inkpen to be
identified as the authors of this work have been asserted
by them in accordance with the Copyright, Designs and
Patents Act 1988.

First published 1988 by Hodder and Stoughton Children's Books
(now Hodder Children's Books)
Paperback edition first published 1990
This Edition published 1996
11 12 13 14 15 16 17 18 19 20

ISBN 0 340 52036 1

Published by Hodder Children's Books
a division of Hodder Headline Limited
338 Euston Road London NW1 3BH

Printed in Hong Kong

SPORTS DAY

NICK BUTTERWORTH
AND
MICK INKPEN

Hodder
Children's
Books

A division of Hodder Headline Limited

Hooray! Today is Sports Day.
Sam is training hard. He's eaten all his breakfast
and now he's doing his exercises.
Tracy is still in bed. She says she's saving her
energy for later.

'Good luck,' says Dad as he goes off to work.
Mum is listening for the weather forecast.
'*. . . and later on, showers spreading to all parts.*'

2

It's a lovely afternoon. It looks like the
weatherman was wrong.
Lots of mums and dads have come to watch.
'Welcome to our Sports Day everybody,' says
Mrs Jefferson. But the loud hailer isn't working
properly and nobody can hear.
She gives it a shake and tries again. Still it
won't work.
Mr Bryant, the caretaker, comes to help.
He switches it on.

The first race is for the infants. It's a bean
bag race.
'Stand back behind the line,' says Miss Foster.
'Ready. Steady. Go!'
They're off.
Jeffrey's bean bag has fallen off his head.
Jenny's is slipping off too.
Matthew's won't come off. He's holding it on.

The next race is the wheelbarrow race.
'Now pushers, don't push too hard,' says Miss Foster.
'We don't want any broken wheels.'
David and Jamie are making a lot of noise.
            'We're being a space buggy, Miss,'
        says Jamie.
            'Spacemen need to be extra careful,'
        says Miss Foster.
                Away they go!
                    Everybody shouts and cheers.
                It's going to be close . . .
                        At the finish the space buggy
                        is just beaten by a
                        wheelbarrow.

Karen has to use special walking sticks to help her get about. She's going to run in the fifty metres dash. Miss Foster says that Karen can start a little in front if she likes. But Karen doesn't want to.
They're off and running.
Look at Karen go! She's going to come third.
Go on Karen!
There's a great big cheer as she crosses the line.
After the race everyone wants a go with Karen's walking sticks.

Sam and his friend Richard are revving up at the
starting line like two racing cars. Brrrmmm!
They're in the egg and spoon race.
Miss Foster says, 'Go!' and they're off.
The girls are going very carefully. Especially Tania.
She isn't going to be first. But she isn't going to
drop her egg.

Sam is doing well. Very well. He's going to win!
'Oh no!' Richard has dropped his egg and it's broken!
It's run all over his shoe.
One of the teachers wipes it off.
'Your mum was supposed to
give you a hard-boiled
egg,' she says.

Oh dear. Where have those clouds come from?
It looks like the weatherman was right after all.
Let's hope it's just a passing shower.
On go the coats. Up go the umbrellas.
Tracy's mum didn't bring an umbrella.
But she did bring a flask.
'Would you like some Miss Foster?'
'Thank you,' says Miss Foster. 'It's brightening up
a bit now.'

Good. The rain has stopped. The sun comes out and
the umbrellas start to steam.
Tracy is in the next race. It's the obstacle race.
'Run backwards to the hoops,' says Miss Foster, 'then
through the hoops, under the sheet, into the sacks
and hop to the finish.'
'Are you ready? Go!'

Tracy's off to a good start.

Oh dear. Joanne's got the hoop stuck.

Tracy's the first one under the sheet.

Matthew's found a hole in it.

Now what's happening?

There's a lot of wriggling and giggling under the sheet.

But no one's coming out.

'I think we'd better help them out,' says Miss Foster.

No one wins. But it was good fun.

The last race of the afternoon is the dads' race.
'My dad's a brilliant runner,' says Henry.
'So is mine,' says Paul.
The dads are all laughing as they wait for the start.
'Go!'
They're off. Oops! Henry's dad has lost a sandal.
Nicola's dad wins. Henry's dad is last.
'Don't cry Henry,' says Miss Foster.
But Henry says he's just got
something in his eye.

And now it's time to go home.
'Well done everybody,' says Mrs Jefferson, and she
thanks everyone for coming. But no one can hear.
Mr Bryant has put the loud hailer away.

'Did you see me win, Mum?' says Sam.
'I certainly did,' says Mum.
'Look, there's Dad!' shouts Tracy. 'Come on Sam.
I'll race you to the gate!'